Managing Green Mandates

Local Rigors of U.S. Environmental Regulation

Pietro S. Nivola

Jon A. Shields

D1609474

AEI-BROOKINGS JOINT CENTER
FOR REGULATORY STUDIES

Managing
Green Mandates

Managing Green Mandates

Local Rigors of U.S. Environmental Regulation

Pietro S. Nivola
Jon A. Shields

AEI-Brookings Joint Center for Regulatory Studies

WASHINGTON, D.C.

2001

l,C, pam,

BIB ID: 283763

Managing Green Mandates: Local Rigors of U.S. Environmental Regulation may be ordered from:

HC
110
.E5
N58
2001

Brookings Institution Press
1775 Massachusetts Avenue, N.W.
Washington, D.C. 20036
Tel.: 1-800-275-1447 or 1-202-797-6258
Fax: 202-797-6004
www.brookings.edu

Library of Congress Cataloging-in-Publication Data

Nivola, Pietro S.
   Managing green mandates : local rigors of U.S. environmental regulation / Pietro S. Nivola and Jon A. Shields.
      p.   cm.
Includes bibliographical references.
   ISBN 0-8157-0233-7 (pbk. : alk. paper)
   1. Environmental policy—United States—Costs. 2. Environmental policy—Economic aspects—United States. 3. United States—Economic policy—Environmental aspects. 4. Environmental economics—United States. I. Shields, Jon A. II. Title.
   HC110.E5 N58 2001
   363.7'056'0973—dc21   2001003261

9 8 7 6 5 4 3 2 1

Typeset in Berkeley

Composition by Cynthia Stock
Silver Spring, Maryland

Printed by Edwards Brothers
Lillington, North Carolina

Contents

Foreword

This volume is one in a series commissioned by the AEI-Brookings Joint Center for Regulatory Studies to contribute to the continuing debate over regulatory reform. The series will address several fundamental issues in regulation, including the design of effective reforms, the impact of proposed reforms on the public, and the political and institutional forces that affect reform.

Many forms of regulation have grown dramatically in recent decades—especially in the areas of environment, health, and safety. Moreover, expenditures in those areas are likely to continue to grow faster than the rate of government spending. Yet, the economic impact of regulation receives much less scrutiny than direct, budgeted government spending. We believe that policymakers need to rectify that imbalance.

The federal government has made substantial progress in reforming economic regulation—principally by deregulating prices and reducing entry barriers in specific industries. For example, over the past two decades consumers have realized major gains from the deregulation of transportation services. Still, policymakers can achieve significant additional gains from fully deregulating other industries, such as telecommunications and electricity.

While deregulating specific industries has led to substantial economywide gains, the steady rise in social regulation—

which includes not only environmental, health, and safety standards but many other government-imposed rights and benefits—has had mixed results. Entrepreneurs increasingly face an assortment of employer mandates and legal liabilities that dictate decisions about products, payrolls, and personnel practices. Several scholars have questioned the wisdom of that expansion in social regulation. Some regulations, such as the phaseout of lead in gasoline, have been quite successful, while others, such as the requirement for safety caps on aspirin bottles, have led to increased risks. As those regulatory activities grow, so does the need to consider their implications more carefully.

We do not take the view that all regulation is bad or that all proposed reforms are good. We should judge regulations by their individual benefits and costs, which in the past have varied widely. Similarly, we should judge reform proposals on the basis of their likely benefits and costs. The important point is that, in an era when regulation appears to impose very substantial costs in the form of higher consumer prices and lower economic output, carefully weighing the likely benefits and costs of rules and reform proposals is essential for defining an appropriate scope for regulatory activity.

The debates over regulatory policy have often been highly partisan and ill informed. We hope that this series will help illuminate many of the complex issues involved in designing and implementing regulation and regulatory reforms at all levels of government.

ROBERT W. HAHN
ROBERT E. LITAN
AEI-Brookings Joint Center for Regulatory Studies

Managing Green Mandates

Government policies to protect the environment in the United States have been largely successful. Twenty-five years ago, only a third of the lakes and rivers in the country were safe for swimming and fishing; today two-thirds are. Almost every toxic waste site was hazardous a quarter century ago; today one-third have been cleaned up. Scores of urban air sheds that were deteriorating in 1970 now are much improved: smog has declined by a third, even as the number of miles driven in motor vehicles has more than doubled; carbon monoxide levels have fallen by almost two-thirds; acid rain has diminished by 40 percent; soot particles are down by more than one-quarter since 1988; and poisonous airborne lead has all but disappeared. The nation's forested acreage is expanding, and the threat to wildlife has diminished in many areas. Americans even are consuming less water than they did fifteen years ago, despite a growing population.[1]

That success has come at a price. A conservative estimate of the costs of complying with the nation's stringent environmental laws in 1990 was that they absorbed approximately 2 percent

The authors are grateful for the comments of Christopher Foreman, Robert Hahn, Mary Graham, Donald Kettl, Robert Litan, Shelly Metzenbaum, and Barry Rabe on earlier drafts of this work. The authors remain solely responsible for its content, which does not necessarily reflect the views of the AEI-Brookings Joint Center for Regulatory Studies.

1

of gross national product, but some studies suggest a considerably greater "environmental drag."[2] The toll in the form of lagging growth in productivity, and hence in workers' wages, has been especially heavy for a number of major industries. Those negative effects notwithstanding, there is little doubt that over time society has netted a gain from most environmental protection programs. Americans are better off with them than they would have been without them.

That's good news. Even better news, however, would be to learn that the hundreds of billions of dollars spent each year on pollution abatement are delivering the biggest bang for the buck. Here, the story gets murky. Many U.S. antipollution rules confer net benefits but do not maximize them. The cost of the rules often is needlessly high; alternative means could secure approximately the same gains with considerably less pain.

Cost overruns have resulted from four distinctive features of U.S. environmental regulation. First, the regulatory regime still subjects communities to controls that often do not befit local circumstances. Rules that might make sense for Miami may be wasteful for Minneapolis. Second, a number of standards seek, in essence, a risk-free environment, and frequently they run up costs exponentially. A few million dollars may be enough to convert some contaminated, abandoned industrial acreage into a reasonably harmless site for an alternative land use. But if the goal is to create a place so pristine that children playing there can safely eat the dirt, the bill for decontamination skyrockets.[3] Third, the enforcement of environmental laws in the United States remains largely a legalistic and antagonistic process, not a notably flexible and consensual one. Intense mutual distrust between parties, commonly degenerating into pitched legal battles, results in virtually every significant administrative decision being put through lengthy formal proceedings. Sometimes these ordeals seem more filled with billable hours than pragmatism. Fourth, federal policymakers continue to dictate to local governments without compensating them adequately for the expense of complying with the dictates. When strapped for revenues, local communities are left to grapple inefficiently with the fiscal burden of the federal government's unfunded mandates.

This monograph explores each of these four difficulties, first by describing them and their origins more fully. Later we review recent innovations in environmental management, concluding that these developments, however welcome, are insufficient. A final section summarizes our main observations and also suggests some general directions for further reform. Environmental programs, we contend, would be more rewarding if they were less distracted by costly assaults on minor risks and if the hyperactive U.S. legal system did not encourage such distractions. The payoff might also increase if local authorities were granted the latitude and wherewithal to tailor their own solutions to local pollution problems. But achieving fundamental changes of this sort cannot be left primarily to the courts and the Environmental Protection Agency (EPA); rather, much responsibility rests squarely with Congress.

One Size Does Not Fit All

That federal standards ought to be contoured to local conditions has long been acknowledged in theory, but in practice, there have been plenty of conspicuous incongruities.

In 1987, Congress required every municipality to treat stormwater much the same as polluted water discharged from industrial plants. This stricture, appropriate for humid watersheds, is ill suited to arid regions, such as much of the Southwest. Phoenix, which records an average of only seven inches of rainfall a year, nonetheless has to spend large sums each year monitoring the runoff from infrequent rainstorms.[4] On top of this annual operating expense have been added many millions of dollars in capital improvements to bring this city's wastewater treatment plants up to standards established to protect various aquatic organisms—despite the fact that none of the organisms can exist in the region's dry riverbeds.

Similarly, under the Resource Conservation and Recovery Act (RCRA), the Environmental Protection Agency's standards for landfills create unjustifiable costs for some southwestern cities. Double liners for landfills are a reasonable precaution in wet climates in which rainfall can cause pollutants to leach into the water table, but they are less crucial in places where there is little rain. Double-lined sites also may be a waste of money where subsurface soils impede liquid percolation. RCRA compliance for Midland, Michigan, has multiplied unnecessarily the costs of disposing of solid waste; this locality's landfill, which sits on 75 feet of clay, probably is safe with no liner at all.[5]

When the federal government tightened the nationwide standards for sewage treatment plants in 1991, Anchorage, Alaska, was instructed to remove at least 30 percent of the organic waste supposedly present in incoming sewage. Local officials protested the rule for a simple reason: that city's sewers had little or no organic matter to remove. Only after considerable legal scuffling did the Environmental Protection Agency relax its demand.[6]

The Clean Water Act requires all cities to install secondary wastewater treatment plants to remove the remaining 0.1 percent of solids, organic matter, and other traces of contaminants not treated in primary facilities. In 1993, however, the National Research Council of the National Academy of Sciences concluded that secondary treatment, while sensible for landlocked communities, may be an extravagance for many coastal cities.[7] The reason: unlike areas that have confined bodies of water (in which nutrients like nitrogen and phosphorus remaining in wastewater treated by primary plants cause excessive growth

of organisms, degrading water quality), coastal cities are affected by tides that help flush excess organic residue into the
ocean. Although EPA since has waived the secondary treatment requirement in a number of instances, the waivers have
uncertainties. San Francisco concluded that it was simpler in
the long run to build an oceanside secondary treatment plant
than to count on obtaining periodic waivers.[8]

Under the rules of the Safe Drinking Water Act, localities
everywhere have been busy examining their water supplies for
pesticides and other toxic residues that pose substantial risks
only in particular areas. Before it was finally relieved from some
of this duty in the mid-1990s, Columbus, Ohio, found itself
guarding against approximately 40 pesticides, many of which
had long since been discontinued in the vicinity—including
one product used chiefly on pineapple plantations in Hawaii.[9]

The common theme in these anecdotes is the awkwardness
of imposing relatively uniform requirements on communities
across a vast continent that comprises regions with widely varying geographic, climatic, and other features. Inevitably, some
perverse consequences ensue.

New York City, for instance, ran afoul of a national prohibition on ocean dumping of sewage sludge. Banned from disposing of any sludge at sea, the city resorted to squeezing refuse
dry in order to transport it to landfills, a practice that emits
nitrogen-rich effluents that endanger marine life in nearby es-
tuaries.[10] In March 1998 the State of Connecticut sued New
York City for contaminating Long Island Sound.[11]

Required to reduce organic waste in its sewerage by a speci-
fied amount monthly, Anchorage had two alternatives: it could
build new sewage treatment installations at a cost of $135 mil-
lion or engage in legal parries and machinations. The city chose
the second option. It went to court, in the meantime allowing
two local fish-processing plants to dump 5,000 pounds of fish
viscera into the sewer system. The fish waste, which could be

easily filtered through the existing treatment facilities, was then removed. Voilà—Anchorage had met the organic-waste reduction rule!

Perhaps few localities across the country have performed contortions so strange, but reports of others, less curious but more costly, have been common enough, increasing the already steep charges for environmental programs. Consider this one: between 1974 and 1994, U.S. taxpayers poured $213 billion into upgrading municipal wastewater treatment plants. Now EPA predicts that an additional $200 billion will be needed through the year 2014 to bring those plants up to new standards.[12] To that estimate must be added another $132 billion for the replacement of aging plants. The projected total rises to $332 billion—a figure that does not include the soaring increases in operating and maintenance expenses associated with more advanced technologies.

Why it has proven difficult for national policymakers to trim escalating costs by better fitting stipulations to local situations is a question this monograph revisits later.

Zero Tolerance

When the EPA sets standards for controlling pollutants, presumably it assesses the risks the pollutants pose to public health and, when possible, estimates the resources needed to lower those risks. Yet its analyses do not consistently inform the choice of ends and means. Too often targets, timetables, and technologies have been decided upon without regard to whether the perils they are meant to diminish are great or small; indeed, policymaking sometimes has proceeded as if risk should be banished at any price. The median cost of EPA regulations per life saved has been estimated conservatively at $7.6 million annually—far more than the median for regulations issued by Washington's other fabled risk-ridding agency, the Occupational

Health and Safety Administration.[13] The feverish pursuit of environmental purification, sometimes tolerating virtually no margin of health risk, is potentially backbreaking for many municipalities, as well as thousands of businesses.

Thus, when the EPA deployed technology-based standards to further curb effluents from municipal incinerators in 1995, it ordered not only a 45 percent reduction in nitrogen oxides below the limits set in 1991, but also further cuts of 85 percent for mercury emissions and 99 percent for lead and dioxin emissions.[14] Levels of most of these toxic substances already had dropped dramatically: overall lead emissions, for example, were reduced 98 percent between 1970 and 1995. The city of Tampa, which had finished building a state-of-the-art incinerator only ten years earlier, then had to retrofit it with another round of pollution-control equipment costing more than $87 million.[15]

Whether the new incineration standards will bring a marked improvement in public health is debatable. In a review of epidemiological studies of individuals living near city incinerators, the Medical Research Council in the United Kingdom could discern no consistent pattern of ill-health.[16] The finding was noteworthy because the studies surveyed relied primarily on data from the 1970s and 1980s, when pollution controls on incinerators were underdeveloped. Today, after at least a decade of stringent regulation, it would be remarkable if the remaining health hazards from these facilities were impressive—particularly in the United States, where a person's average exposure to poisons such as mercury is now less than half the average in Europe.[17]

Some other rules made pursuant to the Clean Air Act of 1990 also have raised questions. The EPA is charged by law with setting air quality standards that protect the public from "*any* known or anticipated adverse effects" on health.[18] Accordingly, the agency in 1997 promulgated new regulations for fine airborne particulate matter and tightened the existing standard for permissible concentrations of ozone in urban areas. Although a federal appellate court voided the revised rules in May 1999, the remand was appealed and the rules since have been reinstated.[19]

That outcome should have positive consequences for the public health—but the question of *how* positive remains unsettled, at least pending more information. EPA itself has observed that the "relationships" between prolonged exposure to ozone (presumably at concentrations of 0.12 parts per million, the standard before 1997) and lasting damage to respiratory tissue "remain highly uncertain."[20] Although particulates are an acknowledged peril, the National Research Council has stressed that the composition of soot varies greatly from place to place and that actual health effects cannot be inferred solely from generalized measurements of concentrations at stationary outdoor monitors that do not necessarily gauge the incidence of human exposure.[21] And while Congress has continued to bear down on various forms of ambient air pollution, a possibly more serious health problem—the often poor quality of indoor air—has not been made an EPA priority. The EPA's indoor air pollution program represents a paltry 0.24 percent of the agency's budget.[22]

While the extent of the health benefits of the controversial rules have not been determined, the expenditures required to comply with them are large. The Council of Economic Advisers puts the total cost for the ozone standard alone at $60 billion.[23] If the standards stick, they multiply overnight the number of nonattainment areas in the country from 106 to nearly 550, evidently encompassing cities, such as Portland, Oregon, that have striven to be models of environmental awareness.[24]

Further reducing harmful emissions should remain high on the list of the nation's environmental objectives. But, arguably, raising urban air quality standards to the point that even comparatively clean and safe places may have to dig much deeper into their taxpayers' pockets to become still cleaner and safer, especially if the improvement in average local life expectancy turns out to be small, can detract from public health more than enhance it. Regulations that cost more than $15 million per early death averted can actually increase premature mortality by withdrawing resources from medical care and nutrition programs and other investments essential to public health and safety.[25] (In February 2001, when the Supreme Court reviewed the Clean Air Act in the momentous case of *Whitman v. American Trucking Association*, the justices found no statutory basis for requiring the EPA to consider these trade-offs).[26]

The issue of radon in household water became another object of concern in the 1990s. Radon in water, however, is a negligible part of a larger problem: radon leaking into homes from surrounding soil.[27] The health threat from radon in water comes chiefly from inhaling the gas as it evaporates, particularly during showering; the amount that escapes in this fashion is no greater than 2 percent of what already is naturally in the air.[28] No matter; in 1999 EPA proposed a rule requiring water to be far more radon-free than the air. What prophylactic effects such regulations would have and whether they outweighed their costs remained very much in doubt.[29] The EPA evidently fixed on water-borne radon in the absence of a more comprehensive "effective regulatory enforcement vehicle capable of reducing radon to an 'acceptable' level."[30]

For local governments in the United States, one of the starkest examples of an environmental program driven by vehement aversion to risk—and hence beset by unexpected costs—has been the Asbestos Hazard Emergency Response Act of 1986. This law mandates the removal of asbestos from classrooms in the nation's 37,000 school districts. Is the presence of asbestos a health hazard worth regulating across the land? A symposium at Harvard University in 1989 concluded that the risk of dying from low-level exposure to asbestos was approximately

400 times lower than the risk from, say, exposure to passive cigarette smoke.[31] The cost of banning asbestos has been estimated to exceed $123 million per life saved.[32] Moreover, ripping the substance from buildings may increase the volume of airborne asbestos fibers to harmful levels, which can persist for years.

Yet, as if America's distressed urban school systems did not have enough demands on their stretched resources, each has had to divert tens of millions of dollars into renovations to reduce what is by and large a slim health risk. New York City delayed opening its public schools in the fall of 1993 so that classrooms could be inspected for asbestos. The city then spent $100 million on abatement—money that could have gone to a much more pressing safety problem at the time: the insufficient number of security guards.[33]

Adversarial Legalism

A third general characteristic of U.S. antipollution policy has been its litigious undercurrent. U.S. environmental regulators may wish that they could formulate their regulations on the basis of dispassionate scientific deliberation and a search for consensus, but in reality, many of the Environmental Protection Agency's decisions involve intensely adversarial proceedings. How did the EPA arrive at its 1997 edict on airborne particulates? A lawsuit brought by the American Lung Association helped force the agency's hand (*American Lung Association v. Browner*, 1994). When did the EPA step up restrictions on municipal trash incinerators? The move came after a string of suits by environmental groups culminated in a Supreme Court ruling that all ash from incineration qualifies as hazardous waste.[34] Why are cities from Atlanta to San Diego scrambling to rebuild their sewers and treatment plants? Court orders have set strict deadlines, sometimes backed by stiff fines, for adherence to the Clean Water Act. What spurred the federal government to coax and cajole every school district into eradicating asbestos? The unrelenting pressure of legal actions played a major part. In the words of Carol Browner, the former EPA administrator, "litigation is essentially setting the priorities."[35] This activity does more than just enforce statutory schedules; it also directs resources to the pet projects of energetic litigators and sometimes away from larger social needs.

A regulatory process flogged by litigation tends to be expensive, and the expenses involve more than legal bills. Although in certain respects key U.S. environmental statutes are remarkably rigid—for example, effectively enjoining the EPA from weighing the extent of the risk its actions supposedly reduce against the costs they incur—in principle the laws also permit considerable discretion in choosing abatement methods. Yet the actual range of choices is somehow narrowed in the course of implementation, during which cost-effective options often are passed up.[36] With an eye to court tests, players in the game—both the regulators and the regulated—lock onto prespecified technologies: the "devil you know," so to speak, may not cut costs but at least hedges against subsequent legal uncertainties.

In establishing standards, policymakers have erred toward risk-minimizing approaches: Why take chances when an alleged tolerance for practically any margin of danger, no matter how small, can invite legal challenges? Thus, compared with pollution limits in other industrial countries, those in the United States tend to be conservative. U.S. restraints on asbestos, radon, and various common pesticides (Alar, for example) have been far more drastic than, say, Canada's.[37] The Canadian "acceptable daily intake" standard for dioxin is roughly 1,700 times more permissive than the corresponding "virtually safe dose" permitted in the United States. Recently, the EPA raised its estimate of health threats from dioxin. If the new indications of high cancer risk from exposure to this toxic chemical are valid, the Canadian standard may well be too lax.[38] But unless the EPA can establish that there is major cause for alarm, the additional investment Americans will have to make to achieve the near-total elimination of dioxin emissions seems unlikely to attain far more health than the Canadians enjoy.

A regulatory process that turns on frequent legal contests and punitive sanctions in order to implement policy also may end up spinning its wheels because participants whose cooperation is essential to the process become evasive. Nowhere has this unintended consequence been more glaring than in the administration of the Comprehensive Environmental Response, Compensation and Liability Act, otherwise known as Superfund.[39] Under this cumbersome program, all current and past owners of contaminated land, not just the main contributors to its contamination, have been liable for damages and remediation expenses. Fearful of the law's unsparing liability provisions, local lending institutions and developers resist investing in many abandoned industrial and commercial sites.

A recent survey of more than 200 cities by the U.S. Conference of Mayors reported no fewer than 81,000 acres of brownfields, including some undoubtedly entangled in Superfund suits.[40] These sites continue to languish in the inner cities, costing them possibly as much as $2.4 billion in lost property tax revenue each year and opportunities to create as many as 550,000 jobs. Meanwhile policymakers bewail the "sprawl" wrought by businesses that, steering clear of the legal liabilities, opt to locate on virgin acreage in the suburbs.

To be efficient environmental policy needs to enforce the "polluter pays" principle. But a legal system that metes out harsh punishment even to the most minor transgressors is in danger of turning that principle on its head. In the free-for-all of Superfund litigation, primary offenders find an incentive to apportion responsibility by suing third parties, many of whom may account for only infinitesimally small shares of the environmental injury in question. So, in a recent California landfill case, the city of Monterey and twenty-eight other municipalities were hauled into a cleanup settlement and confronted with multimillion dollar charges on the grounds that they, too, had polluted the waste site.[41] How much hazardous refuse had they contributed? A fair estimate was less than 1 percent.

There are other potential drawbacks to regulatory initiatives that, more often than not, wend their way through the courts at the instigation of private litigants. The judiciary has the last word on deadlines and technical issues on which it often lacks expertise.[42] By turns, legal squabbling pressures regulators to require hyperhygenic remedies with unrealistic timetables, or it causes delays in carrying out urgently needed measures. Legalistic enforcement, moreover, not only penalizes laggards; it also may impose heavy fines on communities that are making progress as quickly as they can but not within the appointed time.[43]

Fiscal Hardships

Local polluters, whether private or public, ought to bear financial responsibility for correcting the immediate environmental problems they create—but not if regulators make unreasonable demands.

A company should not be expected to spend many additional millions of dollars cleaning a toxic waste site after it already has been decontaminated sufficiently for children to frolic on it and even ingest bits of the soil for seventy days a year without suffering harm. Yet, there have been such cases.[44] Similarly, local water authorities throughout Wisconsin should not have been compelled to spend significant sums over several years to keep testing for certain radioactive contaminants that, according to long-standing records, were nowhere to be found in the state's water supply.[45]

And should cities be coerced into removing from their water supplies faint traces of herbicides that are essentially harmless in small doses? Federal regulations in the early 1990s set the maximum permissible level of Atrazine in drinking water at three parts per billion. A person has a tiny chance of developing cancer if he or she were to drink liters of water containing that minuscule fraction daily over a lifetime. In 1991, before it was allowed to halt the quest for an Atrazine-free water supply, the city of Columbus was spending an appreciable share of its municipal budget on that exercise.

Nor was it self-evident that California ought to scrap its decentralized testing stations for automotive effluents and replace them with a centralized inspection system. Why ask the state to make such a large investment if it soon would be outmoded as automakers perfected onboard emissions testing sensors and as low-cost computerized tracking of auto emissions became available? In fairness, the EPA gave ground there amid mounting congressional skepticism after 1994.[46]

The trouble with federal impositions such as these, particularly for fiscally strained local governments, is that some are not only immoderate but also unaffordable. In 1994, the city of Los Angeles estimated that federally mandated projects, mostly for environmental protection, were claiming $840 million a year, or about one-fifth of the city's revenues from all local taxes and fees.[47] Three years earlier, New York City's Office of Management and Budget had concluded that mandates of one kind or another absorbed an even larger share of local revenues.[48] A fastidious federal agenda that piles on exactions but that assists in defraying only a diminishing portion of their costs can portend serious hardships, most notably for the nation's overtaxed central cities. The National League of Cities has estimated that the EPA's latest ozone standard alone could drain at least $2.5 billion a year from Chicago's economy and tax base.[49]

Within the share of antipollution expenses borne by the public sector, local governments always have done most of the heavy lifting. But the federal government once substantially aided at least those national programs that required an especially strenuous local effort. The statutory goal of the Clean Water Act, for example, has been to end *all* "discharge of pollutants" into waterways.[50] The Safe Drinking Water Act aims to bar from all potable water scores of potential contaminants, many of which other advanced countries consider impractical to prohibit completely.[51] Aware that attaining such ideals would stretch the financial capabilities of many states, cities, and counties, Congress from 1974 to 1994 appropriated about $96 billion to help renovate basic installations such as municipal wastewater facilities. Federal grants-in-aid represented approximately 45 percent of total expenditures; local authorities more than matched that sum during that period. But federal cost sharing for environmental programs has trended downward over the past two decades, and in recent years local governments have had to come up with more than 90 percent of the funding for wastewater infrastructure.[52]

After 1987, direct federal grants for these improvements were replaced with a revolving loan fund against which localities could borrow at low interest rates. Annual appropriations for this fund, however, have totaled less than $2 billion a year—an amount that is insufficient to finance much capital construction, not to mention the mounting costs of operation and maintenance, which reached $12 billion for local authorities in 1998. Some major cities, including Los Angeles, have concluded that often the loans are not worth applying for because they are too small and entail too much red tape. The outlook for a return to more generous federal contributions is bleak. Despite the significant federal budget surpluses that have been projected, cities appear likely to face additional deep cuts in federal assistance for mandated environmental programs of all kinds.[53]

Meanwhile, new and costly obligations loom for many municipalities. As clean water policy heads into the uncharted realm of regulating nonpoint sources of pollution, city officials worry that they soon will bear the brunt of major purification programs for waterways, even as other, often worse polluters (farms, for instance) remain uncontrolled.[54]

One result of inadequate federal support can be widespread local noncompliance. Hundreds of community water systems continue to violate the drinking water law simply because they lack the financial, technical, or managerial abilities to meet its ambitious requirements.[55] But another, less recognized ramification is that communities are pressured to raise their tax rates—and to reduce the resources allocated to other essential services—in order to pay for Washington's wishes.

While affluent places may remain relatively unscathed, economically hard-pressed jurisdictions suffer. In many old metropolitan centers, for example, the higher taxes, coupled with deteriorating basic services such as schools, increase the exodus of middle-class inhabitants and entrepreneurs and dissuade others from coming to the city to live. Thus, by underfunding its manifold environmental plans for the nation's municipalities, the federal government may worsen the abandonment and blight of numerous core cities and abet the relentless dispersal of people and jobs to sprawling suburban subdivisions. This rapacious pattern of development, in turn, increasingly encroaches on ecologically sensitive areas and complicates efforts to lessen air pollution, including greenhouse gas emissions.[56]

Good Intentions Gone Awry

The defects of many environmental regulations—their standardized application, intolerance of petty risk, legalistic approach, and imposition of disproportionate local burdens—are not political accidents. Each has identifiable reasons, including some well-meaning ones.

The Genesis of Generic Treatment. Business interests, not without justification, often prefer nationwide regulatory standards to a hodgepodge of local rules: broad scope and standardization may lower uncertainty and increase efficiency. The ultimate example, of course, is the commerce clause of the United States Constitution. Were it not for this general prohibition against interference with the free movement of goods and services across state lines, the U.S. economy might be encumbered by fifty separate internal barriers to trade. Even when the choice of uniform standards can seem somewhat arbitrary, there may be much to be said for their simplicity. A current illustration can be seen in comparing the European and U.S. mobile phone markets. Industries in Europe are ahead in this particular telecommunications niche partly because the European Union quickly established a single continent-wide technical standard, whereas wireless service in the United States continues to lag behind in part because companies have to navigate multiple systems.[57]

One might think that all but a few forms of pollution are self-contained, amenable to strictly local solutions. But local variability in pollution control can be problematic. Pollution crosses boundaries. Concentrations of ozone, for example, may blow across hundreds of miles. One region's polluted air contaminates another's water: nearly all of the PCBs flowing into the Great Lakes originate from the air, and an estimated one-quarter of the nitrogen in the Chesapeake Bay derives from polluted air drifting from at least four neighboring states.[58] Hazardous wastes often are transported across state lines. In theory, biological contaminants as well as various chemical toxins in an area's landfills may gradually leach into adjoining watersheds. The rotting garbage at New York City's primary

municipal dump discharges into the tri-state region not only
1 million gallons of polluted water each day, but also large quan-
tities of carbon dioxide and methane, gases that are known
contributors to global warming. Unfortunately, a state whose
acid rain or contaminated rivers flow downstream to neighboring states has little incentive to curtail the spillover for their
benefit.

Compounding the inertia is the ease with which opponents
of desirable policies, as Madison warned in *Federalist 10*, may
capture small polities: Will the one-company town, whose fac-
tory is the local economy's mainstay but also its worst polluter,
take the necessary corrective action? And will jurisdictions
competing for business investment and taxable income not be
tempted to dumb down their respective regulations, perhaps
even engaging in "a race to the bottom"?[59]

These are not idle concerns. For the better part of a decade, the Environmental Protection Agency has been waiting
for the state of Georgia to devise a solution to the extraordi-
nary buildup of smog in the Atlanta metropolitan area. Atlanta has one of the dirtiest coal-fired power plants in the
United States, and levels of nitrogen oxide emissions from
motor vehicles have regularly exceeded EPA caps and projec-
tions. Drivers in metropolitan Atlanta rack up more miles per
vehicle each day than drivers in any other U.S. urban area.[60]
But unlike California, which started moving aggressively to
improve air quality in the Los Angeles basin years ago, Georgia has been slow to act. Only recently has the state begun to
do more than debate a series of proposals.[61] While draconian
steps, such as mandating a four-day work week, were justifi-
ably rejected, so were more modest notions—like charging
for parking spaces and converting to cleaner automotive fu-
els. The latter idea, which implied a modest increase in the
price of gasoline, caused consternation in the Georgia legisla-
ture. Cases of this kind suggest that without federal pressure,

some state and local governments may prove disinclined to undertake even minimal improvements.

Federal mandates that begin with the aim of setting sensible baselines, however, commonly overreach. The process of standard setting becomes politicized as communities and interest groups that bear the brunt of regulations—and that claim to be unfairly disadvantaged by them—lobby to spread their costs to others. The Clean Air Act of 1970 originally cracked down on utilities that burned high-sulfur coal, produced chiefly in West Virginia, Kentucky, Ohio, and Pennsylvania. To regain market share, these states prevailed on Congress to amend the law. After 1977 power plants across the land, regardless of the sulfur content of their fuel, were uniformly required to install smokestack scrubbers.[62] Surely, this coast-to-coast requirement was less a public health imperative than an oblique cross-subsidy to Eastern coal producers.

When environmental standards are nationalized in uncompromising terms, it also is because they are advanced by their advocates as, in essence, legal protections to which all citizens are entitled. The debate on the Clean Air Act, for example, was framed from the outset as a matter of securing everyone's "*inherent right* to the enjoyment of pure and uncontaminated air."[63] Akin to a civil right, a legal warrant to a clean environment ceases to be an aspiration that can be adjusted up or down according to local preferences; it is absolute and universal. There is, in other words, no such thing as a partial "inherent right"; rights are all-or-nothing propositions. And because rights, by definition, belong to everyone equally, they cannot vary by locale.

Further, if environmental protection is a legal prerogative, plaintiffs naturally will lay claim to it in courts of law. The omnipresent prospect of environmental litigation, in turn, may drive intimidated industries to seek shelter by widening the scope of mandates. At least that way the companies might know precisely what is expected of them everywhere, instead of remaining exposed to the case-by-case caprice of local juries.

For example, to preempt a wave of lawsuits from parents and school districts, the asbestos industry joined the campaign for statutory asbestos-removal nationwide.[64]

In a fiercely litigious policy arena, beleaguered state and local officials, too, are apt to take cover under a blanket of federal standards. Invoking "the law of the land," even if it is a blunt instrument, often is a surer defense than trying to explain the nuances of exercises in local discretion. In the proceedings that led to broad directives for safe drinking water, the National Governors Association and various associations representing public water systems pressed for all-encompassing standards that might help insulate local administrators from incessant legal wrangles.[65]

Minimizing Risks. Whatever else may explain the existence of environmental regulations that can claim few, if any, net benefits from eliminating marginal health risks, this much is well known: the EPA's hands are mostly tied by acts of Congress. Indoor air quality may now be a more serious health concern than outdoor air. Overall, nonpoint sources of water pollution, such as the runoff from agricultural herbicides and insecticides and from city streets, now pose a greater ecological risk than do traditional point sources such as the effluents spewing from the drainpipes of industrial plants. But EPA's attention is not focused on these predicaments because they are, for the most part, less systematically addressed by current authorizing legislation. Moreover, the Clean Air Act and other key statutes that are fully in force impede the agency from factoring cost evaluations into the standards it sets. The question, therefore, is how these priorities and constraints arose in the first place.

Particularly during the 1980s and early 1990s, when Democratic majorities in Congress faced Republican presidents, environmental policymaking was conducted in an atmosphere of intense mutual distrust. The executive sought to slow the pace; the legislative branch wanted to accelerate it. Suspecting that Reagan and Bush appointees to the EPA would, if permitted, thwart the agency's mission, Congress proceeded to micromanage it through detailed legislation. Thus, EPA administrators were required by law to resolve highly complex matters under grueling deadlines. The Superfund Amendments and Reauthorization Act of 1986, for instance, included among its 150 deadlines a requirement that the EPA prepare an action plan for radon within two years. Under the amended Clean Air Act, the EPA administrator was ordered to meet a similar schedule for the promulgation of standards for sulfur oxides and nitrogen oxides. In establishing ambient air quality standards, the weighing of risks reduced against costs incurred was discouraged. In the view of many members of Congress, Republican administrations could not be trusted to perform impartial evaluations.

In a number of legislative debates, however, more than mistrust seems to have motivated the participants. Sheer zealotry has played a role: Skilled policy entrepreneurs, aided by frenzied media coverage, zero in on a supposed menace.[66] The issue du jour (radon in tap water, say, or Alar-tainted apples) actually may be of minor consequence compared with other dangers (like foul air in buildings or global warming); nevertheless, through strong emotional appeals, mass opinion and lawmakers are mobilized to purge the designated evil. Sponsors of bills vie with one another for maximal impact; the dynamic takes the form of "speculative augmentation," as Charles O. Jones observed in his definitive study of the 1970 Clean Air Act, through which moderate bills are deemed sellouts and increasingly radical alternatives gain legitimacy.[67] An excitable public intensifies the politically charged atmosphere, making moderation even less likely. By the time Congress was debating the tough new amendments to the Clean Air Act in 1990, for instance, a growing number of Americans had become convinced, erroneously, that the nation's air quality had steadily deteriorated and believed, insouciantly, that "environmental improvements must be made *regardless of cost*."[68]

In part, a combination of scientific advances and continuing uncertainties also permits alarmists to dramatize the dangers of inaction. Increasingly sophisticated technologies have enabled scientists to detect hazardous substances in smaller and smaller concentrations.[69] A possible contaminant measured only in parts per million might be noticed in only a handful of scattered sites. But if the same substance is then discerned in parts per trillion, it suddenly may be perceived as ubiquitous. Its presence, even if presenting a minuscule threat in most places, can suffice to frighten people.

The relatively small risks stemming from involuntary exposure to various kinds of pollution appear to be as much as 1,000 times less acceptable to the public than the much larger known risks associated with voluntary activities such as driving motor vehicles, smoking, and owning handguns.[70] And because the science of risk assessment involves approximations, subject to adjustment, there often is just enough indeterminacy to contribute to a climate of fear. That may be why, for example, the government clings to a goal of zero chloroform in drinking water. And it may be why lawmakers stick to an ultra-cautious emphasis on hazardous waste cleanup, dedicating as much as one-quarter of the EPA budget to a problem that many officials believe has been blown out of proportion but that the public perceives as the most serious environmental threat in the country.[71]

America's environmental regulators may not like the box they are in, but they cannot easily break out of it. "No other country has anything near the national tumult over risk issues that America has," concludes Harvey M. Sapolsky of M.I.T.[72] A political system so responsive to surges of selective public anxiety, heightened by the scare tactics of clever issue-advocates and media hype, cuts policymakers little slack. The governments of other countries are not immune to wild misallocations of resources in their efforts to reduce risk either. The British government, for instance, spends approximately fifteen times more on each life saved through its advanced train protection system than on saving lives through road safety programs.[73] But in general, U.S. political institutions seem exceptionally susceptible. "Elsewhere," Sapolsky writes, "governmental authority is more secure, policy-making proceedings more secretive, and official expertise more respected. There is less opportunity, but also less need, for organized interests to use the public's health fears for political advantage."

Of course, not all of the indifference to cost in the quest to reduce risk is dictated by statute. As already suggested, the need for relief from litigation probably accounts for some of the Environmental Protection Agency's orientation. In a society that gives plaintiffs permission to sue public and as well as private entities over practically any threshold of risk, the likely inclination of bureaucrats is to take refuge in unflinching formal precautions, guidelines that say, in effect, "We can't be too careful"—even if it means sparing the economy no expense.[74]

Adversarialism. Adversaries, confronting what they consider to be an obdurate bureaucracy, ritually challenge the EPA in the courts. But more than the predictable resistance of businesses tangles the EPA's legal thicket.

Congress has placed this agency in a unique bind. By the end of the 1980s the EPA was operating under some 800 deadlines for making rules, to which the Clean Air Act amendments of 1990 added another 55 and the 1996 amendments to the Safe Drinking Water Act ordered 80 more. The misalignment between congressional mandates and the agency's limited resources has left it years, sometimes decades, behind in executing most of its major statutory programs.[75] Inevitably, the delays have precipitated a torrent of legal actions by environmental groups.

The pressure applied by these and other litigants, however, ultimately has deeper roots in American political culture. For centuries, foreign observers have marveled at the frequency with which Americans turn to the courts to rectify virtually any of life's inevitable conflicts and misfortunes. "There is hardly a political question in the United States which does not sooner or later turn into a judicial one," wrote Alexis de Tocqueville in 1835.[76] In the year the Constitution was written, J. Hector St. John Crevecoeur lamented in his *Letters from an American Farmer* the way "our laws and the spirit of freedom . . . often tends to make us litigious." This penchant, he added, enabled even "the most bungling" lawyer to "amass more wealth than the most opulent farmer with all his toil."[77]

Apart from a surplus of lawyers, bungling and otherwise, the most distinctive feature of the U.S. legal system is the ease with which complainants, including those with grievances against public agencies, get their day in court. Provisions for private rights of action are a hallmark of U.S. environmental and consumer protection laws, and federal courts generally have entertained a wide variety of challenges by citizens under the Administrative Procedures Act. In no other advanced country can private stakeholders so readily file suits, not only against corporate miscreants, but also against state and local governments for alleged noncompliance with national regulations and against national regulators themselves for alleged underenforcement.

Energized by such cases, the U.S. judiciary has played a singularly aggressive role in comparison with the magistrates of other countries. The U.S. courts have adopted a "hard look" doctrine vis-à-vis government agencies, increasing the burden on them to explain the rationale for their decisions. And at least until recently the courts became, in R. Shep Melnick's words, "increasingly willing to second-guess agencies on their reading of statutes and their interpretation of evidence," often prodding them to pursue their statutory missions more militantly.[78] In *City of Chicago v. Environmental Defense Fund* the Supreme Court ruled that local governments must treat ash produced from municipal incinerators as hazardous waste, not mere solid waste. Ending a decade-long exemption of municipalities from the EPA's hazardous waste management standards, this 1994 case had the side effect of closing Chicago's waste-to-energy incineration plants altogether. The city then took to trucking all its trash to outlying landfills.

In recent years, some district judges reportedly have begun to limit the standing of environmental suits brought by citizens directly against companies.[79] But while plaintiffs may be collecting fewer punitive awards from firms, citizen suits against municipalities and other public institutions remain common enough. The most recent spate of cases has involved efforts by environmental groups to compel the EPA and the states to delineate the Clean Water Act's so-called total maximum daily loads (TMDL) for the inflow of pollutants into bodies of water.[80]

There is no single explanation for this enduring phenomenon. In some situations, litigation is rife because it appears to be the only means of determining how to carry out imprecise provisions of environmental statutes. The Clean Water Act, for instance, provides little guidance for the regulation of nonpoint sources, apart from stipulating that state agencies designate TMDLs for each waterway. Congress, the EPA, and the states still have to fashion strategies for controlling pollution that involves, in the legal vernacular, a joint and several responsibility. Thus, until the federal courts were asked to intervene, regulators appeared to neglect the dangerous contamination of lakes, rivers, and streams by runoff from streets, farm pesticides, and other diffuse sources.

At a deeper level, however, lawsuits are the weapon of choice for more than purely pragmatic reasons. As Robert A. Kagan of the University of California, Berkeley, has argued, while Americans remain fundamentally suspicious of government authority, they nonetheless expect no end of good deeds from all levels of government.[81] If public servants are not trusted, but a great deal is demanded of them anyway, how are their services to be secured? Coercive suits go from being a last resort to a routine device. The Environmental Protection Agency's every move is monitored, not only by vigilant congressional overseers and industry representatives, but by numerous public interest watchdogs ever poised to bring legal sanctions to bear.

Besides a quest for strict accountability, the "See you in court" tradition reflects, as noted, the notion that the public has a right to protection from environmental risks. Emulating the civil rights movement of the 1960s, groups of all kinds have found it expedient to frame their claims as matters of basic justice. Soon after African Americans and other minorities blazed a trail, women, the elderly, the disabled, public health guardians, and others joined the procession. In Philip K. Howard's words, "Congress began handing out rights like land grants."[82] Today, even irate airline passengers, truckers protesting fuel prices, and subscribers to health maintenance organizations demand not only relief but a "bill of rights." Not the least of the groups expecting "total justice," to borrow the phrase of Stanford University's Lawrence M. Friedman, are contestants in environmental conflicts.[83] In the name of environmental justice, the EPA recently issued interim guidelines that explicitly define the "disparate impact" of polluted land as a violation of civil rights.[84] Needless to say, such alleged violations will be redressed where traditionally other abridged rights are redressed: at the courthouse.

"Shift and Shaft" Federalism. The partnership of the central and local governments that once provided funding for some of the costliest environmental programs has given way to a one-sided relationship in which national policymakers order a full plate of costly projects for local officials to undertake and then leave them the tab. The tendency to "shift and shaft," as the locals say, is more than a straightforward extension of the pol-luter-pays principle; the rationale for bucking costs to local taxpayers derives, in part, from national political developments already described. If, for example, pollution abatement is deemed a solemn right, as opposed to a preference competing with other public values, its advancement all but ceases to be a federal budgetary responsibility. The federal government po-lices infringement of civil liberties and rights, but it does not appropriate funds or distribute grants to affirm those rights; it simply requires every local government to respect and help enforce them. Something like this premise has come to inform the federal role in contemporary environmental management.

In addition, budgetary austerity (at least for discretionary spending) during the 1990s was associated with greater con-gressional use of unfunded mandates. Alice Rivlin noticed the connection early in the decade: "When its ability to make grants declined, the federal government turned increasingly to man-dates as a means of controlling state and local activity without having to pay the bill."[85] Up to a point, the cost shifting could be regarded as financially prudent, not only for the federal fisc, but for the nation. When Washington was more generous, en-vironmental projects, like other public works, could include more pork. A serviceable local facility designed to purify water might come in two models: stripped down or fully equipped with all the options. If the feds were paying the bill, few locali-ties would opt for the cheaper project. Local governments do not print money; to spend, they have to tax. Hence they have a greater stake in holding down costs.[86]

Moreover, as the economy began expanding briskly in almost all regions of the country after 1992, local revenues grew. Some policymakers in Washington had long regarded as intergovernmental "subsidies" the deduction of local property taxes from the federal income tax and the exclusion of interest income earned from various forms of debt at the state and local levels.[87] With many states and some localities running surpluses in the context of a reasonably concerted effort to finally balance the federal budget, there was something to be said for further devolution of costs.

But a good deal of federal mandating is also plainly opportunistic: it enables national politicians to claim credit for cleaning up the environment without incurring, in Princeton professor R. Douglas Arnold's term, "traceable" blame for the tax increases required.[88] If more members of Congress play this card now than in the past, part of the reason is that the objections of local officials seem to carry less weight in the halls of the Capitol. As ties to local party organizations have eroded, the allegiances of members of Congress have moved increasingly beyond parochial matters to the agendas of national lobbies and pressure groups.[89] This delocalization of influence is reflected in the pattern of congressional campaign finance. Whereas candidates once depended primarily on the backing of local constituents and party bosses, the soaring costs of campaigns now force candidates to rely more heavily on external sources. As one measure of the trend, the winners of recent House elections have come to draw upward of 40 percent of their contributions from political action committees—that is, from the funding arms not only of corporate donors but of other well-financed interests with a national presence.

Members of the House of Representatives used to be especially sensitive to the concerns of mayors, county executives, and other notables in their district. Now, representatives, much like senators or presidential candidates, pitch their appeals to a wider audience, including Washington-based advocacy groups. Preceding enactment of the nationwide asbestos-removal law, local administrators worried audibly about its looming costs. Democratic representatives, who led the charge for the mandate, were undeterred. And the Republican opposition never coalesced. Indeed, House Republicans largely joined the cause, stressing that "everyone wants to do the same thing. We want to help children."[90] Local misgivings notwithstanding, the House passed the asbestos bill unanimously.

Local misgivings, in any event, often are feebly or belatedly expressed. Amid great expectations of the immediate benefits of many environmental statutes, awareness of their costs often lags. Regulations based on the statutes take time to develop; the bottom line may not become visible for years. The safe drinking water amendments of 1986 passed with considerable state and local support. Only after the EPA's rules emerged several years later, requiring specific (and enormous) local expenditures, did the law become a controversial intergovernmental issue, and even then, the local backlash was uneven and episodic. More than a few local officeholders can almost always be counted on to welcome, indeed invite, mandatory federal standards. These officials may be playing a two-level game in which the standards are perceived, at least at the outset, as a means of gaining leverage over other local players, including bureaucratic rivals.

Innovations

These observations are not meant to imply that the politics and administration of environmental policies have remained static. Efforts have been made to loosen for local governments certain federal requirements. Beginning in 1995, for instance, EPA officials negotiated with about half of the states to develop customized plans for various kinds of pollution control. These so-called Performance Partnership Agreements (PPAs) are an attempt to substitute performance goals for command-and-control–style programs and to reduce EPA's oversight of the states in exchange for their commitment to achieving the goals. The PPA experiments, now extended to some 40 states, reflect more confidence in the administrative capacity of most states and possibly less anxiety in Washington that local authorities, given the chance, will race robotically to the bottom.

By now even consummate federal paternalists have had to recognize that many state legislatures and agencies have led, not lagged, Beltway politicians in formulating vigorous policies. When the federalization of environmental policies began in 1970, most states were underequipped to deal effectively with the problems they faced.[91] Today, the environmental agencies of the fifty states together employ about 60,000 people, more than three times as many as the EPA. The states also pay most of the expense of environmental programs, and some of their initiatives have inspired national policies. California's vehicle emissions standards predated those of the federal government. Recently, New York adopted the California standards, and Massachusetts soon may follow.[92] The controls on pesticides and hazardous waste in quite a few states exceed (sometimes unduly) those required under federal rules.[93] Since the late 1980s various states have been shifting away from "end of the pipe" controls and toward emphasis on pollution-prevention strategies. Minnesota has been an acknowledged leader, as has Massachusetts, which reports having cut businesses' use of toxic chemicals by more than 40 percent.[94]

It is fair to say that the states have taken the lead in cleaning up or managing hazardous waste, including the disposal of substances such as low-level radioactive waste, which often requires coordination among states. More than forty states have supplemented the federal Superfund with more nimble voluntary programs.[95] In these ventures developers or owners of brownfield sites typically receive positive financial incentives, including varying degrees of liability protection, instead of unending summonses, legal fees, and punitive sanctions. The remediation standards for brownfield projects also are more flexible than those of the federal model; the appropriate level of decontamination is decided case by case, according to what is warranted by the intended land use. In some instances, state (unlike federal) procedures permit interim remedies; not every site has to be permanently restored to a "Garden of Eden," explained a Pennsylvania official.[96] Such provisions have enabled the states to rapidly recycle thousands of sites.

Much of the pressure on the EPA to clamp down on drifting effluents from power plants in the Midwest and Southeast has come from Northeastern states, which argued persuasively that they could not meet air quality standards unless the transboundary emissions of other regions were curbed.[97] A number of these northern states threatened to take their own legal steps against distant utilities if the EPA did not act.

Congress has yet to overhaul all of the troubled Superfund law, but some of the program's travails have eased as its retinue of executors and attendants has progressed along an extensive learning curve. The law was amended in 1986 to introduce mandatory reporting of chemical compounds discharged by firms. Over time, this right-to-know provision has spurred a surprising number of self-initiated cleanups, as companies try to avoid potential public-relations debacles.[98] The EPA has taken some steps to encourage the state voluntary programs; for example, the agency recently agreed with ten states not to raise the bar on the results of their variegated cleanup activities.[99] In the spirit of this concession to local control, the EPA also has inched toward limiting future federal liability for some municipalities participating in the state programs. (A main weakness of the state voluntary-cleanup programs to date is that they have not fully shielded participants from federal liability.)

There are some signs of progress in another realm as well: The Republican-controlled Congress has tried to embed in at least some environmental legislation the balancing of costs and benefits of reducing health risks at the margin. The 1996 amendments to the Safe Drinking Water Act now require the EPA to include these considerations when establishing standards.[100] So do some provisions of the Toxic Substances Control Act and the Federal Insecticide, Fungicide, and Rodenticide Act. Evidently, enough lawmakers had come to understand that overzealous restrictions on pesticides can be a mixed blessing. (Pesticides lower the cost of diets rich in vegetables and fruits. The health benefits of such diets overwhelm the long odds of contracting cancer or other serious ailments from moderate spraying of food plants and trees.)

It may be getting harder for Congress to offload the responsibility of ironing out some of the most confusing commandments in its major environmental statutes, given that the Supreme Court now seems unlikely to take in Congress's laundry. When the original Clean Air Act was enacted, the assumption was that there were thresholds below which pollutants did not adversely affect anyone's health. Advances in epidemiology and the heightened sensitivity of modern monitoring devices, however, have since led to the conclusion that, for at least some segments of the public, no such safe threshold seems to exist with respect to ground-level ozone and particulate matter. Because the EPA is charged by statute with guaranteeing an "adequate margin of safety" that will bar "any" ill-health effect, some jurists have noticed a lack of legislative coherence: short of setting maximal standards, and thus presenting society with possibly stratospheric economic costs, the agency is simply unable to follow the letter of the law. This type of fundamental dilemma eventually may impel Congress to write basic revisions, with or without judicial encouragement.[101]

Policymakers also are aware that environmental regulation in this country has been too rancorous. From time to time, the EPA has tried something called regulatory negotiations ("reg neg"), in which the agency formally convenes interested parties and negotiates agreements, the aim being to elicit the cooperation of stakeholders at an early stage in the formulation and effectuation of rules. EPA's so-called Project XL promised a few companies with superior environmental records greater flexibility in meeting the conditions attached to various permits. In a handful of cases (seventy-five as of 1999), EPA has tried to immunize prospective developers of Superfund sites from liability.[102] A number of federal courts, too, finally have begun to rein in some types of citizen suits.

Nor can it be said that policymakers have been indifferent to the local fiscal onus of the nation's environmental agenda. In 1995 Congress passed the Unfunded Mandates Reform Act, intended to interpose additional checks and balances on the propensity of lawmakers to assign costly tasks to local governments without adequate financial support. To cut compliance costs, the EPA also has endorsed a state trading system for nitrogen oxides as a means of achieving targeted reductions in smog-related emissions. (Evidently, big savings attained by an earlier experiment with marketable allowances for emissions— the trading system for sulfur dioxide—had made an impression.) Conscious that the legal minefield of Superfund was leaving large tracts of urban land vacant and blighted, Congress and the EPA have provided support, albeit modest, for demonstration projects to recover brownfields in more than 100 cities.[103]

Under the EPA's so-called Filtration Avoidance Program, some cities are being permitted to try extraordinarily unconventional plans to protect water quality at reduced cost. In lieu of building the world's biggest filtration plant at a price of perhaps $8 billion, New York currently is attempting to improve its water supply by preventing the degradation of upstate watersheds that feed its reservoirs.[104] The project, covering some 1,500 square miles west of the Hudson River, involves everything from land acquisition and stewardship to revision of various farming practices and the replacement of community sewerage infrastructure, including rural household septic tanks.[105] Although the city is spending many hundreds of millions of dollars on these elaborate efforts, presumably they will be cheaper than the alternative.

Remaining Issues

But these developments do not yet signify a full paradigm shift. The four fundamental shortcomings of the regulatory system— incomplete adjustment to geographic differences, too much concern with marginal risks, a surfeit of contentious legalism, and local overloads—persist and remain wasteful.

A performance standard, like any standard, can still conflict with practicalities on the ground in particular jurisdictions. Recall the strange saga of the sewage treatment mandate in Anchorage. Like other cities, Anchorage was directed to rid itself of organic wastes by 30 percent by whatever technique available. Flexibility as to the *means,* however, did not imply that there also was wiggle room in the standard's desired *end* (the 30 percent reduction), which scarcely took account of conditions in Anchorage. Granted, the city ultimately prevailed in court and saved itself the trouble of constructing a new treatment plant, but the point is that *no* action should have been ordered. The EPA should have exempted Anchorage from the outset, not after slogging it out with the city's lawyers.

Gazing at federal standards for solid waste landfills, officials in Southwestern states such as Arizona must wonder whether the professed devolution of national environmental policy and shift to performance-based approaches has gone far enough. Conditions in that part of the country do not warrant the specifications that are justifiable elsewhere. And in any event, why not encourage, indeed assist, individual states to set their own standards? In all but rare circumstances, any added risks would be borne by the residents of those jurisdictions alone, since leaking landfills seldom spill into adjacent states.[106]

By and large, the same holds for the toxic waste sites currently regulated by Superfund. Logic suggests that federal tutelage in pollution abatement should be stronger for forms of pollution that cross state borders and weaker for those that stay in place. But, notes John D. Donahue of Harvard University, federal authority actually has been weaker under the Clean Air Act and the Clean Water Act than under the Superfund law—this despite the fact that most toxic sites "are situated within a single state, and stay there."[107]

"Similarly," writes Paul R. Portney of Resources for the Future, "for all but a few biological contaminants in drinking water, the risks linked with higher concentrations of most contaminants would be borne only by those who consume the affected water for a lifetime. Why, then, not allow the states, or perhaps even individual communities, to decide how stringently they wish to regulate their drinking water?"[108]

Officials in Massachusetts, an environmentally progressive state, have asked themselves the same question in connection with the Safe Drinking Water Act. The state hoped to fulfill the law's objectives through a plan that relied largely on ozone treatment, pipe replacements, and land use controls. But in 1998 the EPA sued Massachusetts to force the construction of a new filtration system.[109] Granted, some states (Massachusetts included) took their time scraping up the cash to boost their water quality to the latest standards. Substantial state revenues were required, however, to offset decreases in federal aid, and the pace of local tax increases warranted federal forbearance.

"The way the federal-state relationship is evolving, it's still very much a parent-child relationship," remarked a deputy commissioner of the Massachusetts Department of Environmental Protection. "Not only are we being told to clean up our rooms, but we're being told how to clean them up."[110]

From Los Angeles and Seattle to Omaha, Detroit, and New York, similar complaints have been noted.[111] "I have been increasingly frustrated by the current state of federal environmental policy," Gregory Lashutka, the former mayor of Columbus, Ohio, recently testified. "Current environmental regulations," he attested, hinder the ability "to target our limited environmental dollars to gain the greatest amount of environmental protection per dollar."[112] The efficacy of environmental policy, in short, rests in considerable part on independent local judgments. If anything, less interference with those judgments may become increasingly important as environmentalism devotes attention to the preservation of ecosystems.[113] Managing their immense diversity calls for case-by-case evaluation and fewer policy templates imposed by Washington.

Above all, environmental policy in the United States has yet to adapt its priorities to the varying severity of public health risks. Much of the current policy agenda remains inefficient because it continues to divert resources to secondary pursuits while failing to address primary problems, remedies for which could yield a larger social payback. Part of the difficulty here is that regulators still do not conduct, as a matter of course, *binding* comparative risk and cost assessments for the management of environmental hazards. Were the EPA to do so, it might be somewhat less likely to contemplate, say, extraordinarily risk-averse national standards for household lead exposure (which would apply to tens of millions of American homes and post an estimated price of more than $50 billion) at the expense of other valued public aims—like increasing the supply of "affordable" housing.[114]

What about the various endeavors to encourage a less acrimonious style of regulation? There is little evidence that experimentation with "reg neg" has produced less litigated outcomes.[115] At bottom, consensus-building ventures like these founder on a fundamental inconsistency in American administrative law: namely, the demand for both extensive public participation and quick results. The 1990 Clean Air Act, for example, invites the many entities it regulates and serves to play an active role in rulemaking. At the same time the law required the EPA to produce scores of new rules within two years. Participants animated by the prospect of influencing policy will not suddenly fall silent when the clock runs out, particularly if they deem those policies unsatisfactory, premature, or insufficiently "representative." How will such groups vent their frustrations? The favored route remains through the courts.

Maybe an overworked judiciary will gradually reduce the opportunities for litigants on *both* sides of environmental disputes to reopen practically every EPA decision through the legal system. Of late, indications are that the courts have begun to subject to stricter scrutiny environmental lawsuits in which plaintiffs cannot demonstrate any direct economic or physical injury to themselves. Whether this will moderate such suits by the "private attorneys general" in U.S. environmental law, however, remains to be seen.[116] In *Friends of the Earth* v. *Laidlaw Environmental Services* (2000), the Supreme Court recently reaffirmed by a 7 to 2 majority the principle of citizen suits.

It will be up to Congress not only to brake the influence of campaign contributions from corporate lobbies on environmental policymaking but perhaps also to temper the practice of deputizing advocacy groups to represent the commonweal in environmental litigation. To rethink these matters intelligently, however, the legislators also will have to acknowledge the fact that litigation, like nature, tends to fill a vacuum. Major omissions or ambiguities in the coverage of environmental laws—precisely how to handle water pollution from nonpoint sources, for example—invite legal disputation.[117]

As for the strain of mandates on the limited resources of municipalities, it hardly has been offset by small-scale programs such as the EPA's brownfield pilot projects, which typically pass out grants no larger than $200,000. Federal aid for pollution control in general shrank more than 20 percent in inflation-adjusted dollars between 1980 and 1994, and despite growing budget surpluses projected after 1998, the decline has yet to be reversed.[118]

True, appropriators can claim that a good deal of the work on various big-ticket items is nearing completion, hence less federal assistance is needed. An example: by 1988, thanks to substantial federal funding, the number of people in communities receiving secondary or advanced wastewater treatment plants had increased from 4 million to 144 million.[119] Most U.S. citizens today are served by relatively modern treatment facilities. On the other hand, other environmental laws, such as the 1990 Clean Air Act, will have profound budgetary implications for metropolitan areas. The Unfunded Mandates Reform Act has been of only modest significance. The ink was barely dry on this supposed safeguard, when, for example, Congress revised the Safe Drinking Water Act, socking cities with another round of huge and mostly uncompensated costs.[120]

It is still too early to tell whether the enhanced flexibility of "new generation" environmental programs, such as the filtration-avoidance agreement for New York City, ultimately will confer fiscal savings. Nobody knows whether New York will succeed in protecting its reservoirs without resorting to filtration or whether the city will first spend a fortune on unorthodox alternatives only to still be ordered to erect the most expensive water-filtering plant on earth. (A recent lawsuit filed by one of the agreement's public interest signatories signaled that the latter outcome is hardly out of the question.)[121]

With or without a lot of federal money, the amended Safe Drinking Water Act is an example of recent legislation that, if sensibly administered, could yield net gains for American cities and for the general public. But some other pending or proposed interventions seem decidedly unpromising. In a single stroke, stringent standards to achieve lead-free buildings, for instance, could classify much of the housing stock in old city neighborhoods as substandard. A federal rule that could precipitate the premature abandonment of thousands of dwelling units is probably the last thing urban centers need as they struggle to reclaim residents and businesses.[122] The quandary should give pause to environmentalists. Metropolitan regions that lose people and jobs at the core will develop more sprawling settlements at the fringes, a mode of urban growth that increasingly is fraught with potentially deleterious implications for the environment.

Conclusions

Although the U.S. government's formidable campaign for environmental protection can legitimately claim major accomplishments, there continues to be room for improvement. In our view, progress will be made if the next generation of environmental management helps to underwrite more programs that accommodate local needs and if it helps to shield those programs from the threat of litigation. Progress, however, will depend on more than cooperative administrators; it will require action by Congress. In some cases, the legislative remedy could entail greater burden sharing by levels of government; in others, it may mean scaling down the scope of obligations that have been heaped on local communities. The result, in other words, will hinge on how fundamental statutes are reauthorized and their funds appropriated, not just on how well the Environmental Protection Agency and local bureaucracies do their work.

Traces of centralized micromanagement of U.S. environmental policy can still be detected—and they remain awk-
ward in a nation so vast and geographically diverse. Not all
environmental problems spill across jurisdictions. Where they
plainly do not, subnational governments have to be entrusted
with the responsibility for designing their own creative solutions—including the authority to set standards for *levels* as
well as techniques of abatement. Also, no government or
economy has unlimited resources to allocate to stamping out
marginal hazards. Environmental policy needs to focus as cost
effectively as possible on the predominant threats to human
health and ecological balance and to move on when they are
mostly, if not *completely*, under control. Green perfectionism
is unsustainable.[123]

Further, these and other critical issues are complicated by
an adversarial decisionmaking style that has featured, among
other imbalances, nearly unlimited recourse to the federal
courts. Judicial review is an admirable institution of American
government, but there can be too much of a good thing. A
system in which plaintiffs' lawyers and magistrates legislate from
the bench, so to speak, relieves legislators of their central responsibility: to write laws with reasonable clarity.

Illustrating this displacement is the legal tempest that has
swelled at least in part because of congressional ambivalence
about how closely to regulate agricultural runoff. At present,
"policy" consists of a dozen disparate court orders, groping for
ways to construe and enforce the Clean Water Act's TMDL con-
cept. As a recent countersuit in California indicated, it is by no
means transparent to what extent Congress intended this law
to crack down on farming practices that might adversely affect
bodies of water.[124] Until the issue is clarified, lawsuits will attempt to fill the gap.

Finally, many local governments are overextended. One knowl-
edgeable observer summarizes their difficult position this way:

The Clean Water Act required cleanup of municipal waste-water discharges, yet federal wastewater-treatment construction grants were being phased out and replaced by payable loans. The EPA's landfill standards increased the cost of traditional municipal solid waste management methods by as much as ten times, while its new drinking-water standards required more expensive monitoring and purification efforts. Local governments, too, were required to replace their underground fuel tanks, and many school systems were compelled to remove asbestos from ceilings, floors, and insulation. The 1990 Clean Air Act amendments added costly automatic penalties on cities that failed to achieve new compliance timetables; Superfund liability imposed costs to clean up contaminated municipal land-fills, and cities became owners by default of many abandoned industrial sites. Yet local governments had no new [federal] revenues to pay for these tasks, and the laws provided no mechanism for setting priorities among them.[125]

Full federal reimbursement of all these particulars is not defensible. It would create a moral hazard in that states and localities that had intended to take independent action could simply sit back and wait for federal grants. Nor should the nation's taxpayers be asked to foot the bill for isolated pollution crises created by, and harmful only within, a few communities. But when, for example, federal policymakers reach into every community to rid the Republic of what are in most places relatively minor perils, federal preferences should be either funded with federal dollars or scaled back.

Most of the adjustments we have highlighted probably will be made over time, although to what extent and how quickly is hard to say. It is possible, for instance, that state and local governments will see some fiscal relief in future years if, as anticipated, the annual federal surplus continues to pile up multiple hundreds of billions of dollars.[126] As environmental statutes come up for reauthorization or revision, more are likely to abandon the cost-oblivious approach of the past and perhaps even the folly of targeting trivial risks. That, albeit still too timidly, has been the direction in which Congress has been nudging recent legislation such as the Safe Drinking Water Act of 1996. Washington also could continue to concede more local control over some programs, especially as policy almost perforce must diversify to preserve wildlife habitats and highly variable ecosystems.

Maybe even the process of implementation gradually could become less litigious—if the political system ever comes to terms with internal inconsistencies that abet the problem. For example, perhaps all parties should stop exploiting carte blanche to drag the courts into disputes over nonpoint sources of pollution. But to help curb these suits, Congress will have to enter the breach. At a minimum, it ought to cease stimulating the sources of pollution through practices such as subsidizing ethanol farms, underpricing water supplies for irrigation, and encouraging soil-enrichment with fertilizers that increase nitrogen runoff.[127] Such steps may sound modest, but in the real world of American politics they would be bold strides.

Notes

1. See Greg Easterbrook, *A Moment on Earth* (Viking, 1995), and "America the O.K.," *The New Republic*, January 4 and 11, 1999, pp. 19–23. Paul R. Portney, "Environmental Policy in the Next Century," in Henry J. Aaron and Robert D. Reischauer, eds., *Setting National Priorities: The 2000 Election and Beyond* (Brookings, 1999), pp. 361–64. See also Jonathan Rauch, "There's Smog in the Air, but It Isn't All Pollution," *Washington Post*, April 30, 2000, pp. B1, B4.

2. See, for instance, Martin L. Weitzman, "On the 'Environmental' Discount Rate," *Journal of Environmental Economics and Management*, vol. 26 (1994), pp. 200–09. While the bill for direct compliance totaled 2.1 percent

of the gross national product in 1990, Weitzman contends that the actual "environmental drag" may range as high as 4 to 6 percent of GNP.

3. See Stephen Breyer, *Breaking the Vicious Circle: Toward Effective Risk Regulation* (Harvard University Press, 1993), pp. 11–12, 29.

4. Karen O'Regan, environmental programs manager, "Unfunded and Underfunded Mandates," *Phoenix City Council Report,* October 20, 1993, pp. 2–3.

5. Brian O'Neill, National League of Cities, in testimony before the Senate Governmental Affairs Committee, February 24, 1998.

6. Interview with Brian Crewdson, utility management assistant, City of Anchorage, March 15, 2001.

7. National Research Council, *Managing Wastewater in Coastal Urban Areas* (Washington, D.C.: National Academy Press, 1993).

8. The San Francisco example illustrates the kinds of local complications that arise even under EPA policies intended to increase local flexibility. San Francisco had obtained a waiver in the early 1980s, but it was good only for five years. If one day the city would have to build a second treatment plant, a particular site was preferred. Rather than risk that subsequent waiver applications would be turned down and that by then the site would no longer be available, the city broke ground for the new facility in the late 1980s and opened it in September 1993.

9. Interview with Michael J. Pompili, assistant health commissioner, City of Columbus, March 15, 2001. Many years earlier, however, the product in question had been in use near Columbus.

10. Edward I. Koch, "The Mandate Millstone," *The Public Interest,* no. 61 (Fall 1980), p. 48.

11. Mike Allen, "Connecticut Joins Lawsuit over Pollution in Sound," *New York Times,* March 24, 1998, p. A24.

12. Robert F. Lawrence and Elizabeth A. Zelinka, "Regulatory Change Drives Need for Water Investment," *New York Law Journal,* March 8, 1999. Association of Metropolitan Sewerage Agencies, *The Cost of Clean: Water Quality Challenges in the New Millennium* (Washington: March 1999).

13. Tammy O. Tengs and others, "Five Hundred Life-Saving Interventions and Their Cost-Effectiveness," *Risk Analysis,* vol. 15, no. 3 (1995), p. 370. A median figure, of course, scarcely describes the often much higher value placed on health risks implicit in particular EPA regulations. For example, a study of pesticide regulation calculated that $35 million was being spent per cancer case avoided among workers who apply pesticides. Maureen L. Cropper and others, "The Determinants of Pesticide Regulation: A Statistical Analysis of the EPA Decision Making," *Journal of Political Economy,* vol. 100, no. 1 (1992). For a broad review of estimated net cost per statistical life saved under various regulatory programs, including several under EPA's aegis, see Robert W. Hahn, Randall W. Lutter, and W. Kip Viscusi, *Do*

Federal Regulations Reduce Mortality? (Washington: AEI-Brookings Joint Center for Regulatory Studies, 2000).

14. U.S. Environmental Protection Agency, "Standards of Performance for New Stationary Sources and Emission Guidelines for Existing Sources, "*Federal Register* 60 (December 19, 1995), pp. 65378–436. Technology-based standards automatically tie pollution reductions to the maximum reductions that can be attained through available technologies.

15. City of Tampa, *Mayor's Strategic Initiatives* (January 1999), pp. 51–2; Tom Arrandale, "The Big Burnout," *Governing Magazine* (August 1998).

16. Medical Research Council, *Health Effects of Waste Combustion Products* (Leicester, U.K.: University of Leicester, Institute for Environment and Health, 1997).

17. U.S. Environmental Protection Agency, *Mercury Study Report to Congress: Volume II* (December 1997), p. 5-1.

18. 42 U.S.C. 740 (emphasis added).

19. Mathew L. Wald, "Court Overturns Air Quality Rules," *New York Times*, May 15, 1999, p. A1.

20. U.S. Environmental Protection Agency, "Final Rule: National Ambient Air Quality Standards for Ozone," *Federal Register* 62 (July 18, 1997), p. 38859.

21. National Research Council, Committee on Research Priorities for Airborne Particulate Matter, *Research Priorities for Airborne Particulate Matter* (Washington: National Academy Press, 1998), pp. 49, 109–13.

22. J. Clarence Davies and Jan Mazurek, *Regulating Pollution: Does the U.S. System Work?* (Washington: Resources for the Future, April 1997), p. 21.

23. Philip H. Abelson, "Proposed Air Pollutant Standards," *Science*, vol. 277 (July 4, 1997), p. 15.

24. U.S. Environmental Protection Agency, *National Air Quality and Emissions Trend Report 1993* (October 1994), table 5-4.

25. Randall Lutter, John F. Morrall III, and W. Kip Viscusi, "The Costs-Per-Life-Saved Cutoff for Safety-Enhancing Regulation," *Economic Inquiry*, vol. 37, no. 4 (October 1999).

26. In the words of Justice Antonin Scalia, the Clean Air Act "unambiguously bars cost considerations" from the standard-setting process. Excerpted in Linda Greenhouse, "E.P.A.'s Right to Set Air Rules Wins Supreme Court Backing," *New York Times*, February 28, 2001.

27. Tom Arrandale, "A Guide to Environmental Mandates," *Governing Magazine*, vol. 7 (March 1994). Less than 1 percent of deaths from radon occur from exposure through household drinking water. National Research Council, *Risk Assessment of Radon in Drinking Water* (Washington: National Academy Press, 1999).

28. Association of California Water Agencies, *National Primary Drinking Water Regulation for Radon-222* (Sacramento, Calif.: February 4, 2000), p. 1.

29. One recent independent study, using the EPA's own numbers, concluded that the costs of regulating radon in drinking water would exceed the benefits by about $50 million annually. Robert W. Hahn and Jason K. Burnett, *The EPA's Radon Rule: A Case Study in How Not to Regulate Risks* (Washington: AEI-Brookings Joint Center for Regulatory Studies, January 2001).

30. Association of California Water Agencies, *National Primary Drinking Water Regulation,* p. 8.

31. John D. Spengler and others, *Summary of Symposium on Health Aspects of Exposure to Asbestos in Buildings* (Cambridge, Mass.: Energy and Environmental Policy Center, John F. Kennedy School of Government, Harvard University, August 1989). A 1989 article in the *New England Journal of Medicine* found no excess cases of cancer from low-level exposure. See Brooke T. Mossman and J. Bernald L. Gee, "Asbestos-Related Diseases," *New England Journal of Medicine,* vol. 320, no. 26 (1989).

32. Robert N. Stavins, "Environmental Protection: Visions of Governance for the Twenty-First Century," Working Paper (Cambridge, Mass.: John F. Kennedy School of Government, Harvard University, June 23, 1998), p. 22. The figure is in 1994 dollars.

33. National School Boards Association, *A Survey of Public Education in the Nation's Urban School Districts* (Alexandria, Va.: 1995).

34. *City of Chicago* v. *Environmental Defense Fund,* 114 Sup. Ct. 1588.

35. Rich Henderson, "Green Eyeshades," *American Enterprise,* vol. 6 (January 1995), pp. 83–4.

36. See in general, David Wallace, *Environmental Policy and Industrial Innovation: Strategies in Europe, the U.S., and Japan* (London: Earthscan Publications, for the Royal Institute of International Affairs, 1995), p. 124.

37. Kathryn Harrison and George Hoberg, *Risk, Science, and Politics: Regulating Toxic Substances in Canada and the United States* (Montreal: McGill-Queen's University Press, 1994), chap. 9.

38. Gina Kolata, "E.P.A. Scientists Find Greater Cancer Risk in Dioxin," *New York Times,* May 18, 2000, p. A24.

39. Some 20,000 lawyers have been actively engaged in Superfund litigation. Marc Landy and Mary Hague, "The Coalition for Waste: Private Interests and Superfund," in Michael S. Greve and Fred L. Smith, eds., *Environmental Politics: Public Costs, Private Rewards* (Praeger, 1992), p. 78.

40. U.S. Conference of Mayors, *Recycling America's Land: A National Report on Brownfields Redevelopment,* vol. 3 (February 2000), pp. 9–10. A principal reason, cited by fully 78 percent of the cities surveyed, for why brownfields lie fallow is "liability issues."

41. Antonio Olivo, "Carwashes Get Huge Bill from Superfund Site," *Los Angeles Times,* October 19, 1998, p. A1.

42. See, in general, R. Shep Melnick, *Regulation and the Courts: The Case of the Clean Air Act* (Brookings, 1983).

43. As one of many examples, the EPA recently joined a lawsuit filed by a local environmental organization citing the City of Los Angeles for allowing sewage to be flushed too frequently into streets, rivers, and the Pacific Ocean (*Santa Monica Baykeepers* v. *City of Los Angeles*, 1998). City officials were understandably perplexed by the timing of the action. Six hundred million dollars already was being spent to improve L.A.'s sewer lines, and the city planned to add another $1.4 billion over the next ten years. Reportedly, Los Angeles was well below the national average in number of spills per mile, even though the city's collection system was the largest in the country. Moreover, inasmuch as the spillage problem involved stormwater discharge, it had been compounded temporarily by the El Niño rains of 1998. The normally dry city did not call for the precautionary system of storm drains that cities in wetter climates do. What repairs the Los Angeles sewers did require already were under way. (Whether the city will face significant fines as a result of this litigation remains to be seen. It may be noted that when the EPA negotiates enforcement penalties, it sometimes allows a community's penalty payments to revert to the community. A sizable share of payments collected during the cleanup of Boston Harbor, for example, was put into a trust fund managed by the state for the harbor.)

44. This is not an apocryphal example. In one case, *United States* v. *Ottati & Goss*, involving a waste dump in New Hampshire, a company spent an additional $9.3 million to settle a suit after the contested site already was deemed clean enough for children playing there to eat small amounts of dirt daily for seventy days a year without suffering any significant harm. See Breyer, *Breaking the Vicious Circle*, pp. 11–12, 29.

45. U.S. General Accounting Office, *EPA and the States: Environmental Challenges Require a Better Working Relationship*, GAO/RCED-95-64 (April 1995), p. 5.

46. See Arnold M. Howett and Alan Altshuler, "The Politics of Controlling Auto Air Pollution," in Jose A. Gomez-Ibañez, William B. Tye, and Clifford Winston, eds., *Essays in Transport Economics and Policy* (Brookings, 1999), pp. 242–43.

47. Report from City Administrative Officer, "Impact of Federal and State Unfunded Mandates and Recommendations for Action," City of Los Angeles, June 17, 1994, p. 1. Los Angeles's total revenue receipts in 1997–98 were slightly more than $4 billion. City of Los Angeles, *1997–98 Budget Summary*.

48. Scott Minerbrook, "The Cratering of New York," *U.S. News & World Report*, vol. 110 (May 27, 1991), p. 31.

49. Paul Bailey, "New Air Standards: A Poor Bargain for Americans," *Nation's Cities Weekly*, vol. 20 (February 3, 1997), p. 14. For other impressive estimates of the costs of the ozone standard for various cities, see Randall Lutter, *Is EPA's Ozone Standard Feasible?* (Washington: AEI-Brookings Joint Center for Regulatory Studies, December 1999).

50. 33 U.S.C. 1251

51. Robert Ballard and Karen M. Keating, "Is There an Ocean of Difference? A Comparison of the European Community's and the United States' Environmental Regulations Protecting Air and Water Quality," *Villanova Environmental Law Review*, vol. 5, no. 1 (1994), pp. 148–49.

52. Association of Metropolitan Sewerage Agencies, *The Cost of Clean*.

53. Frank Shafroth, "City Priorities on Block Even amid 'Surplus,'" *Nation's Cities Weekly*, March 29, 1999.

54. On municipal concerns over pending implementation of TMDL obligations and the unbalanced financial responsibilities they may impose, see John Millet, "Impending Clean Water Mandates May Unfairly Target Cities," *Nation's Cities Weekly*, April 12, 1999, and testimony by Rudy McCollum, vice chair of the National League of Cities, before the Subcommittee on Water Resources and Environment of the House Committee on Transportation and Infrastructure, June 22, 1999.

55. U.S. General Accounting Office, *Safe Drinking Water Act: Progress and Future Challenges in Implementing the 1996 Amendments* (Government Printing Office, January 1999), p. 12.

56. For a discussion of these issues, see Pietro S. Nivola, *Laws of the Landscape: How Policies Shape Cities in Europe and America* (Brookings, 1999).

57. See Edmund L. Andrews, "Next Stage of the Cellular Tour: As Europe Zooms Ahead, U.S. Fiddles with Formats," *New York Times*, July 27, 1999, p. C1.

58. See Mary Graham, *The Morning After Earth Day: Practical Environmental Politics* (Brookings, 1999), p. 80.

59. Susan Rose-Ackerman, "Does Federalism Matter? Choice in a Federal Republic," *Journal of Political Economy*, vol. 49, no. 1 (1981), pp. 152–63. Also, John H. Cumberland, "Interregional Pollution Spillovers and Consistency of Environmental Policy," in M. Siebert and others, eds., *Regional Environmental Policy: The Economic Issues* (New York University Press, 1979), pp. 255–81.

60. David Goldberg, "Heads Up, Atlanta: Cities Are Scrambling to Comply with the Clean Air Act's Strict New Rules," *Planning*, vol. 64 (July 1998), p. 20.

61. By the mid-1990s, Southern California, which had long harbored the nation's worst smog, had the cleanest air in forty years. Smog alerts diminished from 121 in 1977 to seven in 1996.

62. See Bruce A. Ackerman and William T. Hassler, *Clean Coal/Dirty Air: Or How the Clean Air Act Became a Multibillion-Dollar Bailout for High-Sulfur Coal Producers and What Should Be Done about It* (Yale University Press, 1981).

63. These were the words of the bill's sponsor, Senator Edmund Muskie (D-Maine). Senate Committee on Public Works, *A Legislative History of the Clean Air Amendments of 1970*, 93 Cong. 2 sess., Committee Print, 227, 231 (emphasis added).

64. Paul L. Posner, *The Politics of Unfunded Mandates: Whither Federalism?* (Georgetown University Press, 1998), p. 87.

65. Posner, *Politics of Unfunded Mandates*, p. 84.

66. Beginning in the 1970s, public interest advocates and their congressional allies became a match for their K-Street counterparts and for business sympathizers. Only now, owing to Republican control at both ends of Pennsylvania Avenue, has the balance of power shifted, some might say lurched, to industry lobbies.

67. Charles O. Jones, *Clean Air: The Policies and Politics of Pollution Control* (University of Pittsburgh Press, 1975). More generally, see also Aaron Wildavsky, *But Is It True? A Citizen's Guide to Environmental Health and Safety Issues* (Harvard University Press, 1995).

68. See James Q. Wilson and John J. DiIulio Jr., *American Government: Institutions and Policies*, 7th ed. (Houghton Mifflin, 1998), p. 655 (emphasis added). Even today, according to recent opinion polls, more than two-thirds of the public subscribe to the statement: "Despite the Clean Air Act and Clean Water Act, air and water pollution seem to continue to get worse." Rauch, "There's Smog in the Air, But It Isn't All Pollution." *Washington Post,* April 30, 2000, p. B4.

69. Walter A. Rosenbaum, *Environmental Politics and Policy*, 4th ed. (CQ Press, 1998), p. 143.

70. See Rick Weiss and Gary Lee, "Pollution's Effect on Human Hormones: When Fear Exceeds Evidence," *Washington Post*, March 31, 1996, p. A14. A thousandfold increase in people's aversion to involuntary risks compared with voluntary ones has been observed in a number of studies. In general, individuals appear to have great difficulty differentiating between extremely low-probability events and ones that may be as much as 100 times more likely to occur. See W. Kip Viscusi, *Fatal Tradeoffs: Public and Private Responsibilities for Risk* (Oxford University Press, 1992), p. 150.

71. Howard Kunreuther and Paul Slovic, "Science, Values, and Risk," *Academy of Political and Social Science,* vol. 545 (May 1996), p. 117, and Davies and Mazurek, *Regulating Pollution,* pp. 20–5.

72. Harvey M. Sapolsky, "The Politics of Risk," in Edward J. Burger Jr., ed., *Risk* (University of Michigan Press, 1990), p. 93.

73. "The Price of Safety," *The Economist*, November 25, 2000, p. 19.

74. Related to this point, see Harrison and Hoberg, *Risk, Science, and Politics*, pp. 50, 171. Early on, the EPA invoked formalized cancer-risk models to support its regulations for DDT and other pesticides. Sheila Jasanoff, *The Fifth Branch: Science Advisors as Policymakers* (Harvard University Press, 1990), p. 182.

75. In the words of former EPA administrator William Ruckelshaus, "Any EPA official will tell you that the agency has the resources to do not much more than 10 percent of the things Congress tells it to do." Quoted in J.

Clarence Davies and Jan Mazurek, *Pollution Control in the United States: Evaluating the System* (Resources for the Future, 1998), pp. 19–21. On statutory deadlines see Norman J. Vig and Michael E. Kraft, eds., *Environmental Policy in the 1990s*, 2d ed. (CQ Press, 1994), pp. 131–32, and U.S. General Accounting Office, *Safe Drinking Water Act: Progress and Future Challenges in Implementing the 1996 Amendments* (GAO), p. 7.

76. Alexis de Tocqueville, *Democracy in America*, J. P. Mayer and Max Lerner, eds. (Harper and Row, 1966), p. 248.

77. Quoted in Charles Warren, *A History of the American Bar* (Buffalo: William S. Hein, 1990), p. 217.

78. Melnick, *Regulation and the Courts*, pp. 9–12.

79. William Glaberson, "Novel Antipollution Tool Is Being Upset by Courts," *New York Times*, June 5, 1999, p. A1.

80. As of this writing, environmental groups have won court orders compelling the EPA to secure state TMDLs in 13 states. Complaints or notices to sue have been filed in 21 additional states. See U.S. Environmental Protection Agency, Office of Water, *TMDL Litigation by State* (January 1999).

81. Robert A. Kagan, "Adversarial Legalism in American Government," *Journal of Policy Analysis and Management*, vol. 10, no 3. (1991), pp. 369–406. For a broad treatment of private rights of action see Peter H. Schuck, *Suing Government: Citizen Remedies for Official Wrongs* (Yale University Press, 1983).

82. Philip K. Howard, *The Death of Common Sense: How Law Is Suffocating America* (Random House, 1994), p. 61.

83. Lawrence M. Friedman, *Total Justice* (Russell Sage Foundation, 1988).

84. On environmental justice, see Christopher H. Foreman Jr., *The Promise and Peril of Environmental Justice* (Brookings, 1998).

85. Alice M. Rivlin, *Reviving the American Dream: The Economy, the States and the Federal Government* (Brookings, 1992), p. 107.

86. On how devolution has been a cost-control mechanism for social programs such as Medicaid, see James R. Tallon Jr. and Lawrence D. Brown, "Who Gets What? Devolution of Eligibility and Benefits in Medicaid," in Frank T. Thompson and John J. DiIulio Jr., *Medicaid and Devolution: A View from the States* (Brookings, 1998), p. 237.

87. James R. St. George, "Unfunded Mandates: Balancing State and National Needs," *Brookings Review*, vol. 13 (Spring 1995), p. 14.

88. R. Douglas Arnold, *The Logic of Congressional Action* (Yale University Press, 1990).

89. See Pietro S. Nivola, "Sweet and Sour Pork: Or Why Regulating Is More Succulent than Spending," paper prepared for delivery at the Annual Meeting of the American Political Science Association, August 28–31, 1997, Washington, D.C.

90. Republican congressman William Goodling quoted in Posner, *Unfunded Mandates*, p. 101.

91. Portney, "Environmental Policy," p. 378.

92. Richard Perez-Peña, "New York to Set Tough New Limits on Auto Emissions," *New York Times,* November 7, 1999, p. A1.

93. Margaret Rosso Grossman, "Environmental Federalism in Agriculture: The Case of Pesticide Regulation in the United States," in J. Braden and others, eds., *Environmental Policy with Political and Economic Integration: The European Union and the United States* (Cheltenham, U.K.: Edward Elgar, 1996), pp. 274–304. David J. Lennett and Linda E. Greer, "State Regulation of Hazardous Waste," *Ecology Law Quarterly,* vol. 12, no. 2 (1985), pp. 183–269.

94. "Reducing Toxics Use and Emissions: State Aids Industry to Cut Pollution and Costs," in *Innovations in American Government 1999* (Ford Foundation, 1999), p. A4. See also the excellent overview of state activities in Barry G. Rabe, "Power to the States: The Promise and Pitfalls of Decentralization," in Norman J. Vig and Michael E. Kraft, eds., *Environmental Policy,* 4th ed. (CQ Press, 2000), especially pp. 35–40.

95. U.S. General Accounting Office, *Hazardous Waste Sites: State Cleanup Practices,* GAO/RCED-99-39 (December 1998). See also U.S. General Accounting Office, *Superfund—State Voluntary Programs Provide Incentives to Encourage Cleanup,* GAO/RCED-97-66 (April 1997).

96. Alexander Volokh, "Shades of Green," *Reason,* vol. 30 (May 1998).

97. Steve Twomey, "Court Upholds EPA in Fighting Dirty Air Crossing Boundaries," *Washington Post,* March 4, 2000, p. A4.

98. See Portney, "Environmental Policy," pp. 375–76.

99. GAO, *Superfund,* p. 39.

100. U.S. General Accounting Office, *Safe Drinking Water Act: Progress and Future Challenges in Implementing the 1996 Amendments* (January 1999). How well the benefit-cost analysis has been performed in *practice* for recent rules, such as the radon issue, is another matter. See Hahn and Burnett, *The EPA's Radon Rule.*

101. On the various points in this paragraph, consult Randall Lutter and Christopher DeMuth, "Wizards of Ozone," *Weekly Standard,* June 21, 1999, pp. 17–19. See also James Wilson and J.W. Anderson, "What the Science Says: How We Use and Abuse It to Make Health and Environmental Policy," *Resources,* vol. 128 (Summer 1997); Rosenbaum, *Environmental Politics,* pp. 143-44.

102. Charlene Crabb and Cathy Cooper, "Building on Brownfields," *Chemical Engineering,* vol. 105 (December 1998).

103. Crabb and Cooper, "Building on Brownfields."

104. Rough cost estimate suggested in interview with John R. Murray, assistant director, Office of Management and Budget, New York City, December 4, 2000.

105. United States Environmental Protection Agency, Region 2, *Assessing New York City's Watershed Protection Program: The 1997 Filtration Avoidance*

Determination, Mid-Course Review of the Catskill/Delaware Water Supply Watershed (May 2000).

106. Portney, "Environmental Policy," p. 379

107. John D. Donahue, *Disunited States* (Basic Books, 1997), p. 65.

108. Portney, "Environmental Policy," p. 379.

109. Graham, *The Morning After Earth Day,* p. 97. In May 1999, a federal district judge in Boston seemed to concur with the Massachusetts Water Resource Authority, which argued that the alternative strategy of ozonation, chlorination, and pipe replacement would better serve the objectives of the amended Safe Drinking Water Act (providing a degree of state discretion in how to achieve maximum protection of the public health) than would the EPA's insistence on filtration. An appellate ruling on the lower court's opinion, however, is pending.

110. Margaret Kriz, "Feuding with the Feds," *National Journal,* August 9, 1997.

111. Tom Arrandale, "The Price of Potability," *Governing,* December 1997.

112. Gregory Lashutka, mayor of Columbus, Ohio, in testimony before the National Science Board's Task Force on Environment, March 9, 1999.

113. See on this point Richard Pouyat, "Science and Environmental Policy: Making Them Compatible," *BioScience,* vol. 49 (April 1, 1999).

114. The original proposal was to affect 57 million housing units at an estimated cost of at least $52 billion, according to the EPA. The EPA's final standards were even more stringent. For a thorough critique that identifies excess costs, see Randall Lutter, *An Analysis of the EPA's Proposed Lead Hazard Standards for Homes,* Working Paper 99-5 (Washington, D.C.: AEI-Brookings Joint Center for Regulatory Studies, May 1999). The average level of lead found in the blood of humans in the United States already had declined by 78 percent from 1976 to 1991. See also Davies and Mazurek, *Regulating Pollution,* pp. 10, 18.

115. Graham, *Morning After Earth Day,* p. 101. Some of the vagaries of EPA's experimental programs (the XL program, for example) have been bizarre. EPA turned down the 3M Company's bid to participate, for instance, although 3M already was emitting less pollution than permitted by law. Minnesota officials who helped develop the company's proposal felt that federal regulators were going overboard. "EPA wanted the company to go through a torturous kind of process to track their performance," one official concluded. "In the end, it came to the point where there wasn't really all that much flexibility." Kriz, "Feuding with the Feds."

116. Michael S. Greve, "Environmentalism and Bounty Hunting," *The Public Interest,* vol. 97 (Fall 1989), pp. 15–29.

117. Litigation is likely to intensify as a result of the EPA's recent rules for implementing nonpoint source controls through state-administered total maximum daily load plans. Matthew L. Wald and Steven Greenhouse, "E.P.A.

Institutes Water Regulations before a Bill Blocking Them Becomes Law," *New York Times*, July 12, 2000, p. A14.

118. See Michael E. Kraft and Norman J. Vig, "Environmental Policy from the 1970s to the 1990s: An Overview," in Norman J. Vig and Michael E. Kraft, eds., *Environmental Policy in the 1990s*, 3d ed. (Washington, CQ Press, 1997), p. 18. In constant 1997 dollars, all federal spending on natural resources and the environment in 1998 remained below the level in 1980. Vig and Kraft, *Environmental Policy*, 4th ed., p. 396.

119. Davies and Mazurek, *Regulating Pollution*, p. 15.

120. The source water assessment program in the law, which aims to prevent groundwater contamination, requires state and local authorities to assess every public water system in the nation—a total of more than 170,000 systems.

121. Winnie Hu, "Group Says City Fails to Keep Its Part of a Clean-Water Pact," *New York Times*, June 28, 2000, p. B4.

122. See in general, Lutter, *Analysis of the EPA's Proposed Lead Hazard Standards*.

123. American policymakers might take a page from the European Union's approach to certain environmental problems. Whereas the stated purpose of the U.S. Clean Water Act, for instance, is to *eliminate* "the discharge of pollutants into navigable waters," the Europeans take the position that policy should "prevent, reduce, and *as far as possible* eliminate pollution" of waterways (emphasis added). This less utopian goal would seem to enable regulators to go about their work pragmatically, laboring under fewer potentially unrealistic expectations, including court-ordered deadlines. See Ballard and Keating, "Is There an Ocean of Difference?" pp. 148–49.

124. In 1999 the American Farm Bureau Federation filed suit against the EPA in *Pronsolino et al.v. Marcus*, C-99-1828.

125. Richard N. L. Andrews, "Risk-Based Decisionmaking," in Vig and Kraft, *Environmental Policy*, p. 222.

126. Congressional Budget Office estimates. Richard W. Stevenson, "Uncle Sam Learns Thrift While America Spends," *New York Times*, July 4, 1999, p. WK 5.

127. Pervasive underpricing of water in the United States is the kind of low-profile perversity that ought to receive much more attention in policy circles. Robert N. Stavins of Harvard writes that at least one-third of the 60,000 public water systems in the country subsidize waste by offering volume discounts, and even among the 22 percent of utilities that charge higher rates for those who use more, prices typically are set far below the social costs of the water supplies. Robert N. Stavins, "How to Stop Squandering Water? Raise Its Price," *New York Times*, August 14, 1999, p. A13.

JOINT CENTER

AEI-BROOKINGS JOINT CENTER FOR REGULATORY STUDIES

Director
Robert W. Hahn

Codirector
Robert E. Litan

Fellows
Robert W. Crandall
Christopher C. DeMuth
Randall W. Lutter
Clifford M. Winston

In response to growing concerns about the impact of regulation on consumers, business, and government, the American Enterprise Institute and the Brookings Institution established the AEI-Brookings Joint Center for Regulatory Studies. The primary purpose of the center is to hold lawmakers and regulators more accountable by providing thoughtful, objective analysis of existing regulatory programs and new regulatory proposals. The Joint Center builds on AEI's and Brookings's impressive body of work over the past three decades that evaluated the economic impact of regulation and offered constructive suggestions for implementing reforms to enhance productivity and consumer welfare. The views in Joint Center publications are those of the authors and do not necessarily reflect the views of the staff, council of academic advisers, or fellows.